DATE DUE

FEB 8 '92		
AUG 3 '92	OCT 03 '9	
SEP 1 4 92	FEB 1 4 '96	
DEC NOV 0 9 92	APR 1 4 '97	
	5-28-9	
NOV 1 7 92	JA 30 9	
MAR 0 9	JUL 20 9	
JUN 0 3 9	DEC 1 6 9	
NOV 19 '93	MAR 24 '99	
MAY 1 3 '95	APR 13 '99	
	6-1-99	
	JUN 04	

+
392.36
Hu   Huntington, Lee Pennock.
          Simple shelters / by Lee Pennock Hunting-
      ton ; illustrated by Stefen Bernath. -- New
      York : Coward, McCann & Geoghegan, c1979.
          63 p. : ill.

          Y. Dwellings. I. Bernath, Stefen. II. Title.
      78-23712   [A] B M
                                            301.54

ABOUT THE BOOK

Food and shelter have always been primary human concerns. In early cultures, the way people obtained their food—by hunting, by herding, or by farming—was one of the factors that decided what kind of shelter was required. A second decisive factor was climate. A third was the availability of materials for construction. Other influences, which varied enormously from one society to another, were family patterns, religion, and tradition.

In this book it is possible to include only some of the many kinds of shelters found in various geographical regions. The examples you will find here were chosen because they illustrate certain basic types, ranging from the most primitive kind of protection from the weather to carefully planned and constructed buildings. They represent the development of elementary architectural forms utilizing a diversity of materials. They demonstrate also how the life-styles of the builders influenced the design of their shelters.

Our ancestors knew the elements of house building because they were the builders. Now, in our technological age, many people have no direct involvement in the construction of their homes, for many of today's houses are far more complex than those early dwellings. But with the growing awareness that our natural resources are not infinite, we are beginning to look with more respect upon simpler ways of life. The shelters of older cultures, built of local materials, relate closely to their environment and the real needs of the people who lived in them. The variety of solutions developed in the past to meet the need for shelter is a striking demonstration of what human ingenuity can do in collaboration with nature, using only materials provided by the earth.

SIMPLE SHELTERS

by LEE PENNOCK HUNTINGTON
illustrated by STEFEN BERNATH

Coward, McCann & Geoghegan, Inc.   New York

General editor: Margaret Farrington Bartlett

Text copyright © 1979 by Lee Pennock Huntington
Illustrations copyright © 1979 by Stefen Bernath

Library of Congress Cataloging in Publication Data

Huntington, Lee Pennock.
  Simple shelters.
  SUMMARY: Describes basic types of shelters found in
different geographical regions of the world.
  1. Dwellings—Juvenile literature. [1. Dwellings]
I. Bernath, Stefen. II. Title.
GN414.H86   1979   301.5′4   78-23712
ISBN 0-698-30690-2

PRINTED IN THE UNITED STATES OF AMERICA

For
STEPHANIE
and those she shelters:
Natalie,
Emma,
and
Maël

CONTENTS

When you have finished, you have a fine place all your own. Who cares if the walls are a little crooked and the floor full of splinters? You have a place where you can eat, sleep, read, visit with your friends, or just sit quietly thinking.

Outside are rain, wind, snoopy people, and whatever wild beasts happen to be prowling around the neighborhood.

Inside there is you, warm, dry, and safe.

Every living creature needs shelter.
Birds make nests; some animals dig tunnels, others burrow in hollow logs.
Human beings use their hands and brains to build many kinds of shelters.
Shelter is a place to be protected
from the weather . . .
a place to be safe from enemies . . .
a place to be private . . .
a place to take care of babies . . .
a place to store food . . .
a place to sleep.

INTRODUCTION

A tree house is a simple shelter you can make yourself. First you pick a sturdy tree, and climb up to choose a place to build in the strongest branches. Then you look around for what you can find to build your house. Some boards; a hammer and nails. Maybe some pieces of tin for a roof, some lengths of rope for a ladder.

Now you set to work, lifting things into place, pounding them together. If you have friends to help, the work goes quickly.

9

Thousands of years ago, people often lived in caves. Stones were piled across the front of the cave to keep out wild animals. Inside, the cave people could keep a fire going, and there was space to store meat and fruits.

Cave dwellers were hunters. Sometimes they needed to travel far to follow the herds of animals that moved around searching for fresh grass and leaves. During these hunting trips, the hunters built themselves temporary shelters. They stuck poles into the ground and held them in place by stones. They cut saplings or branches to make walls. In the center of the hut pebbles marked the place for a cooking fire.

The hunters did not stay in these shelters very long. They wanted to get back with meat for their families waiting in the home caves.

Later, people discovered that instead of going hunting they could domesticate certain wild animals. They began to keep herds of cattle, sheep, and goats. Now they could count on a steady supply of meat, wool, and hides. Instead of gathering whatever they could find growing wild, they began to plant their own wheat or rice or maize. Some people still hunted, but many others became farmers or shepherds.

All around the earth people began making different kinds of housing. Farmers built homes where they expected to stay a long time. Shepherds and hunters built temporary shelters they could move with them or leave behind.

11

How did people first decide what kinds of shelters to build?

What are the things you have to think about before you build?

First, the climate.

Is it hot where you live? Or cold? Very rainy? Or very dry? Whatever the weather, your shelter must give protection from it.

A second important thing is the kind of materials you can find to make your shelter.

The earth can supply many kinds of materials for building.

Are there trees growing nearby that you can cut for wood? Are there stones you can use for supports and walls? Are there reeds or vines you can weave? Is there clay soil that can be mixed with water to make mud bricks? Or snow that can be made into building blocks?

A third thing to think about is how you will be using the house.

Some families like to live by themselves. Others like to have a great many relatives living together in an extended family. Some people like to live in a house away from others, some want to live in houses built close together in a village.

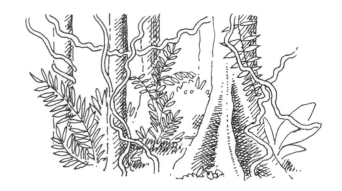

Builders must think too about the shape of the house.

Will it be a round house? A square or a rectangle? Will it have a flat roof? A pitched roof? A dome? The roof has to be strong enough to bear the weight of rain or snow and the force of the wind.

Will the walls be high or low? The walls will have to be strong enough to hold up the roof. Between the walls there must be additional supports for the roof. These also help hold the building together.

People have solved these problems in different ways in different places. They have used their imaginations to make houses that are sensible for their climates. They have developed ways to use materials they could find right where they wanted to live. And they have built houses to suit the kinds of living patterns they have chosen.

When you make a wall or put on a roof, even just for a tree house, you are doing something that has been done millions of times before by people all over the earth. When you sit inside the shelter you have made, you have the feeling of safety and comfort that people everywhere want to feel in their homes.

IGLOOS

In the Arctic, far to the north, where the land is covered with ice and snow most of the year, live the Caribou Eskimos. They are hunters, wandering across the frozen land in search of seals, caribou, polar bears, and fish. During the short weeks of summer, grass grows on the flat plains called the tundra, but there are no trees. The Eskimos live in summer tents made of skins.

In winter the violent winds can make the temperature drop as much as a hundred degrees below zero. To shelter themselves during the Arctic winter the Caribou Eskimos build an

14

igloo, a house of snow. An igloo is shaped like a hemisphere, or half a ball. The low round shape is better than a square house in the Arctic because the wind blows over it in a curve instead of striking full force against a high flat wall.

Building an igloo is a little harder than you might think. First the Eskimo must find the right kind of snow. It has to be hard and deep, not soft or powdery. He digs a round pit about ten feet wide in the snow. Then with his long narrow knife he cuts blocks of snow about three feet long, two feet wide, and a foot thick. He sets them in a circle around the edge of the pit. The Eskimo stands inside the circle to work.

He shapes more snow blocks and fits them on top of each other. Each row is tilted slightly inward and is smaller than the one below. The blocks placed in a continuous spiral make a dome shape. When the last block is put in place at the top of the dome, the cracks are filled with loose snow. The Eskimo cuts his way out of the dome by making an opening that will be the doorway.

A hole is cut over the doorway and a piece of ice is put in place to make a window. A trench is dug outward from the door and roofed over with packed snow, making a tunnel entrance. A curved wall is built to protect the entrance. The Eskimo can crawl in and out of the tunnel, but the wind cannot rush directly through into the igloo.

Inside the igloo are platforms of packed snow

for sitting and sleeping. Caribou hides make warm, soft covers. When it is dark, a seal oil lamp is lit. Seal oil is used for cooking, too, although Eskimos eat much of their food raw or dried rather than cooked. A small cooking fire gives off enough heat to help keep the Eskimo family comfortable, but it does not get hot enough inside the dome to melt the solid icy walls. The Eskimos sitting together in a circle feel warm enough to take off their fur parkas even when the wind howls outside and the snow piles up deeper and deeper. The children listen to the stories their parents tell of fishing and hunting adventures, and the baby sleeps soundly. Everyone is safe and warm in a shelter made of snow.

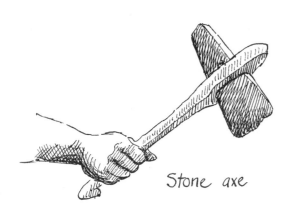

Stone axe

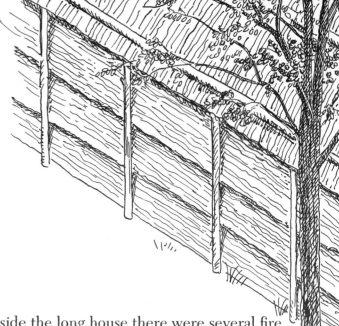

LONGHOUSES

In North America, some Indian tribes have lived in permanent villages and some have been nomads. When the Pilgrims came to New England, they found villages with fields of maize—what we call corn—and pumpkins where Indian women tended the crops while the men fished or went hunting in the forests.

Among the Iroquois Indians, some had their settlements in the northeast region we now call New York State. Several families would live together in a large building called a long house. It had a frame of wood with a high rounded roof. Elm bark covered the whole outside in overlapping pieces like big shingles. There was a doorway, but there were no windows.

Inside the long house there were several fire pits in the central space. These were used for cooking and for warmth during the long cold winters. Along the walls were wooden platforms for sleeping and storage. Big boxes made of bark held maize. More maize was stored outside in covered pits in the ground. An open space in the village was kept for dances to celebrate a victory in battle with another tribe, or to give thanks to the gods, animals, and plants for providing food.

When the land close to the village wore out and no longer produced good crops, and firewood became scarce, the whole village moved to a new place and built a new community of long houses.

TIPIS

On the great prairies that extend for hundreds of miles across North America, Blackfeet, Crows, Dakotas, and other tribes of Plains Indians hunted buffalo. Buffalo were hunted not only for their meat. Every part of the animal was useful. The skins with hair left on made heavy winter clothing. Hides with hair scraped off were made into shirts, leggings, and moccasins, or cut into strips for ropes. Buffalo hair was used to stuff pillows. Sinews (the tough tissues between muscle and bone) were made into thread, the bones into knives, and the horns into spoons and needles. Buffalo hides also provided shelter. They were made into tents called tipis.

It took at least twelve buffalo hides to make one tipi. The Indian women sewed the skins together in the shape of a half circle, using bone needles. Then the women stood up three or four poles and tied them together near the top. More poles were set around to make a circle. The hide cover was tied tightly along one pole and then pulled around the circle and tied again. The bottom of the cover was held down by pegs or stones. Two flaps at the top could be opened for a smoke hole or closed tightly to keep out wind and rain. The doorway was just an opening in the hide at the front.

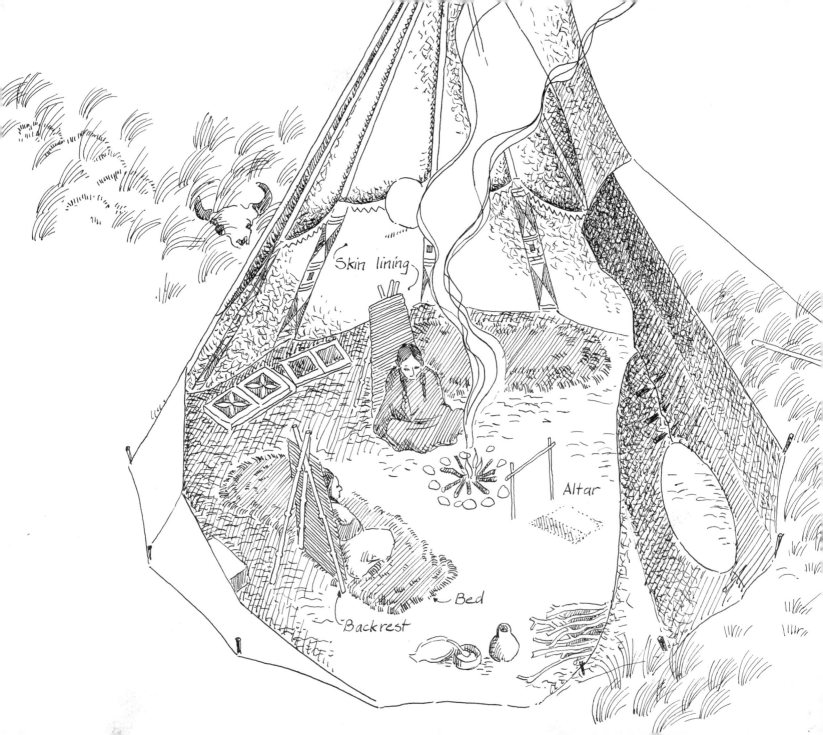

Skin lining

Altar

Bed

Backrest

Inside, the tipi was lined with more hides to keep out the wind. Flat stones in a circle made the fire pit in the center. Dried grass covered with soft buffalo hides made places to sit or sleep. Outside and inside, the tipi was decorated with painted patterns or picture stories of hunting.

The tipi could be taken down and moved when the hunters followed the buffalo herds to new feeding grounds. The hide cover was wrapped around the poles and loaded on a wooden drag frame harnessed to a dog or a horse.

Tipis were homes for the Plains Indians for many hundreds of years. When the white men came with guns and killed almost all the buffalo, the Indians could no longer hunt. There were no more buffalo hides to make tipis.

NORTHWEST COAST CEDAR HOUSES

On the northwest coast of North America, the mountains come down almost to the Pacific Ocean, and great forests of pine and cedar grow tall in the year-round rain and fog. For hundreds of years Tlingit, Klamath, and Haida Indians fished in these waters and lived along the seashore or near rivers in villages of thirty or more large wooden houses, each shared by several families.

Even though their tools were only of stone, shell, and bone, the Indians could cut and carve big cedar trees. Cedar wood is strong and long-lasting, but easy to carve. Sections of

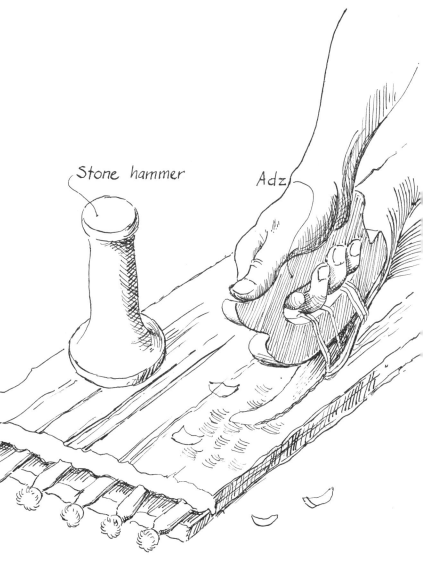

Stone hammer

Adz

Stone chisel

Wood wedges

trunks were used for the frameworks of the houses. The roofs sloped down and were covered with curved cedar planks that carried off rainwater. The outsides of the houses were covered with wide flat cedar planks. During the summer, the Indians sometimes took off these planks, loaded them on canoes, and took them along to where they would be fishing for a time. There the planks were used to make small summer houses. When winter came, the planks were brought back to the main village and put in place again on the sides of the big houses.

Inside each house against all the walls were banks of earth. These were used as shelves for fur blankets, wooden bowls, and supplies of dried berries and fruits. Mats were hung from the ceiling to separate family sections.

Outside the door stood tall posts carved with the designs of birds or animals chosen by the families of that house. These brightly painted totem poles guarded the houses in summer when the people were away fishing and in winter when the people stayed inside making canoes and feasting.

PUEBLO INDIAN VILLAGES

In the dry southwest of North America there are many mesas, or flat-topped mountains. Some Indians live in villages on the mesas. When Spanish settlers came, they called these villages by the Spanish name of pueblos, and the Indians came to be known as Pueblo Indians. These Indians grow maize, melons, pumpkins, and beans wherever they can find springs of water.

Pueblo houses are built next to each other like apartment buildings. Sometimes they are five stories high and have entrances reached by outside ladders. Some pueblos are built of stone, others of adobe. Adobe is mud that has been shaped into bricks and dried in the sun. The bricks are used to make very thick walls that keep the rooms cool during the hot summer and warm during the winter months.

Heavy pine beams are laid on top of the adobe walls. Sticks and brushwood are laid across the beams, then a layer of clay is spread over the brushwood. The Indians stamp this clay with their feet until it is smooth. The clay dries very

Maize

Store Room

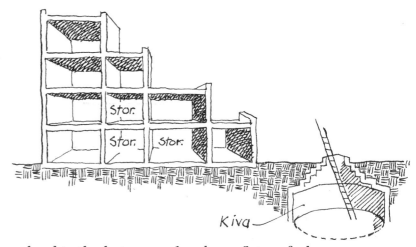

Kiva

Grinding stone

hard in the hot sun and makes a flat roof where the Indians like to sit and work. Pueblo Indians are skilled craftsmen and make beautiful woven baskets, pottery, and patterned cloth.

Instead of doors, some rooms in the pueblo have holes in the roof. To get in, you must climb up one ladder outside and down another inside. The rooms are very small and usually have stone floors. Each family lives mostly in one room, with its own cooking fire and stones for grinding meal. A special room holds supplies of maize.

Each Pueblo village has a kiva, a large underground room for ceremonies. In the kiva are pictures made of colored sand with designs of sun, moon, stars, and animals. The pictures are offerings to the spirits, who are asked to bring rain, good crops, and good health to all the people of the pueblo.

31

AMAZON RIVER HOUSES

In South America, groups of Indian families live in small clearings in the jungle along the Amazon River. The Boro Indians use one very large house shared by everyone in the community.

Tall tree trunks are felled by burning to make a frame for the house. Rafters for the roof are made of branches tied to the frame with vines. Folded palm leaves are tied to the roof frame to make a thatch a foot thick, sloping down almost to the ground. The low walls are covered with mats. The house looks like a big circus tent, and is big enough to shelter fifty or more people.

Each family has its own place inside, with a separate fire pit where pots of soup are always kept bubbling. Everyone has his own hammock for sleeping. The center part of the house is kept clear for meetings and dancing. Near the house, trees are cut and burned to make space for gardens where manioc, an edible root, is grown, along with maize, beans, and sometimes bananas. The men fish in the river and hunt in the jungle with spears and blowpipes.

After several years of constant heavy rains, the roof of the big house begins to leak badly. The Boro Indians do not repair their house. They simply move to a new clearing and build another house and start new garden patches.

NEW GUINEA
STILT HOUSES

Halfway around the world there are other places where it rains nearly every day. In New Guinea, an island north of Australia, people live along rivers where they fish. They build wood-frame houses with heavy thatched roofs like the Boro Indians, but they place their houses on stilts high above the ground so that they will not be flooded. A ladder must be climbed to get in the door.

Bamboo, a tall plant with tough, jointed stems, grows thickly in the moist soil. The New Guineans cut strips of bamboo to make walls for their stilt houses. The bamboo is woven loosely enough to let in some air, because it is always warm. But mosquitoes find their way in too, and people have to sleep inside big bags made of tightly woven reed mats so the insects won't bite them.

Fire pits

Sleeping bag

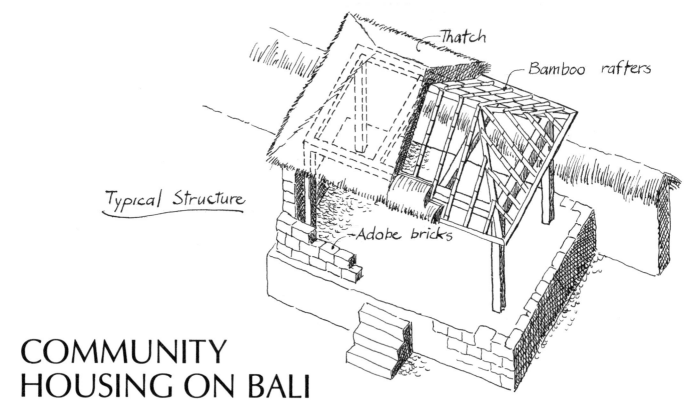

Typical Structure

Thatch

Bamboo rafters

Adobe bricks

COMMUNITY HOUSING ON BALI

On the island of Bali in Indonesia, people live near their rice fields in houses of mud brick with bamboo rafters and thatched roofs. Each family group makes its own shelter on a separate piece of land. Every married couple in the group has a little one-room house to sleep in with their children. One building is used as a kitchen by all the wives of the extended family, but each wife has her own cooking fire there.

There is also a house where guests can sleep, and another area serves as a family temple.

Old people, parents, children, dogs, and roosters all live together inside a double wall. If you are a visitor coming in the gate of the outer wall, you will find a second wall running part way along the inside. The entrance to the inner wall is not opposite the main gate but around a corner. This is to keep out evil spirits. The tradition is that evil spirits cannot turn a corner, so this is the way to keep them out of the family living spaces.

Bamboo grove

FARM HOUSES IN INDIA

In Asia there are many kinds of climate and different kinds of shelter. In India, where many farmers grow rice, it is nearly always hot, and during the season of monsoons, rain comes down in torrents. The rain is good for the rice, which is grown in water-covered fields called paddies.

The rice fields are plowed by cows and water buffalo. Along the paddies grow stands of bamboo and palm trees with large, tough leaves. The Indian farmers use materials that are right there for their building: mud, bamboo, palm leaves, rice stalks, and cattle dung. They make house frames of bamboo. Bricks are made of mud mixed with rice straw. Roofs are covered with palm-leaf thatch. Walls are plastered with dung to make a hard, dry surface.

People try to build their houses on high ground, so they will not be flooded in the monsoons. The house is usually a small square, just one room for the whole family and a shed for the cow. But nearly every house has a garden with pumpkins, yams, and melons.

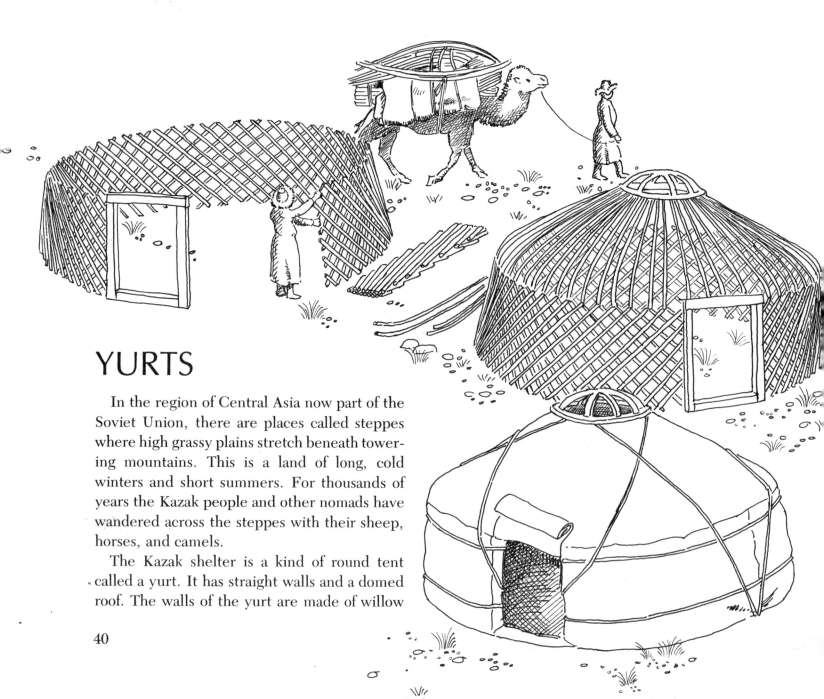

YURTS

In the region of Central Asia now part of the Soviet Union, there are places called steppes where high grassy plains stretch beneath towering mountains. This is a land of long, cold winters and short summers. For thousands of years the Kazak people and other nomads have wandered across the steppes with their sheep, horses, and camels.

The Kazak shelter is a kind of round tent called a yurt. It has straight walls and a domed roof. The walls of the yurt are made of willow sticks tied together with leather strips in a pattern called a lattice. A lattice can open up wide or close into a narrow space.

When the Kazaks are traveling, the lattice frames are closed into bundles which can be loaded on camels or horses. When it is time to stop and put up the yurt, the lattices are opened out and joined together in a circle. The dome, made of willow sticks like umbrella ribs, is fastened onto the lattices. Then the yurt is covered with felt, a very heavy material made from sheep's wool. In the summer, only one layer of felt cloths is used. In winter, as it gets colder, more layers of felt are tied on.

Inside there is a brazier in a fire pit at the center of the yurt. Smoke goes up through a hole in the top of the dome. Colorful rugs are spread around for sitting and sleeping. Clothes are stored in leather bags. The baby, in a cradle hung from the wall like a hammock, is warm and safe with the family inside the yurt.

Brazier

Sour Mare's milk bag

Cooking pot

BUSHMEN HUTS

In Africa people build their shelters in many different climates. Places where it is hot and dry, or hot and rainy, places where it is very cold at night even though the sun burns fiercely all day long, and high places with strong winds. There are jungles, grasslands, deserts, and mountains.

In southern Africa, on the edges of the Kalahari Desert, days are hot and nights cool. Hunters called Bushmen live in this rugged region and in the nearby swamps. Bushmen spend almost all their time looking for food and water. They move around following animals such as giraffes and ostriches, which they catch in snares or shoot with poison-tipped arrows. The women dig for edible roots and gather berries, fruits, and insects, which are eaten raw.

Bushmen make a very simple shelter by piling twigs and grass over a frame of sticks. The front of the hut is left open, with the cooking fire on the ground just outside. Empty gourds are used as pots and drinking water is kept in ostrich egg shells.

Water hole

When the animals move to a fresh water hole, the Bushmen abandon their huts and make new ones in the new hunting grounds.

43

DESERT TENTS

The vast Sahara Desert stretches across the North African countries of Morocco, Algeria, Tunisia, Libya, Mauritania, Mali, Niger, and Chad. Many of the Bedouin and Berber people who live here are nomads, leading their herds of cattle and camels, sheep and goats, across the desert in search of food and water.

These nomads take their tent homes with them. Their desert tents do not have the tall conical shape of Indian tipis. They are low and broad to provide the most shade under the blazing desert sun. The sides may be left open during the day when it is hot, or closed when the desert wind blows furiously and at night when the temperature suddenly drops and the air becomes bitterly cold.

Some desert tents are made of leather from cattle hides. Others are woven strips of the hair of sheep, goats, or camels. Some tents are made of mats or leaves from palm trees. The frame of the tent is wood. Since few trees grow in these dry sandy places, wood is precious and the tent frame is always taken along when the family moves.

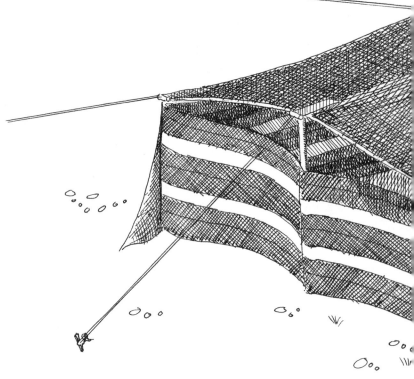

With a few clay pots and some woven mats for beds, the nomad family has all it needs to make a home which can be easily taken down, loaded on a camel's back, and carried along, to be put up again quickly at the next stopping place.

44

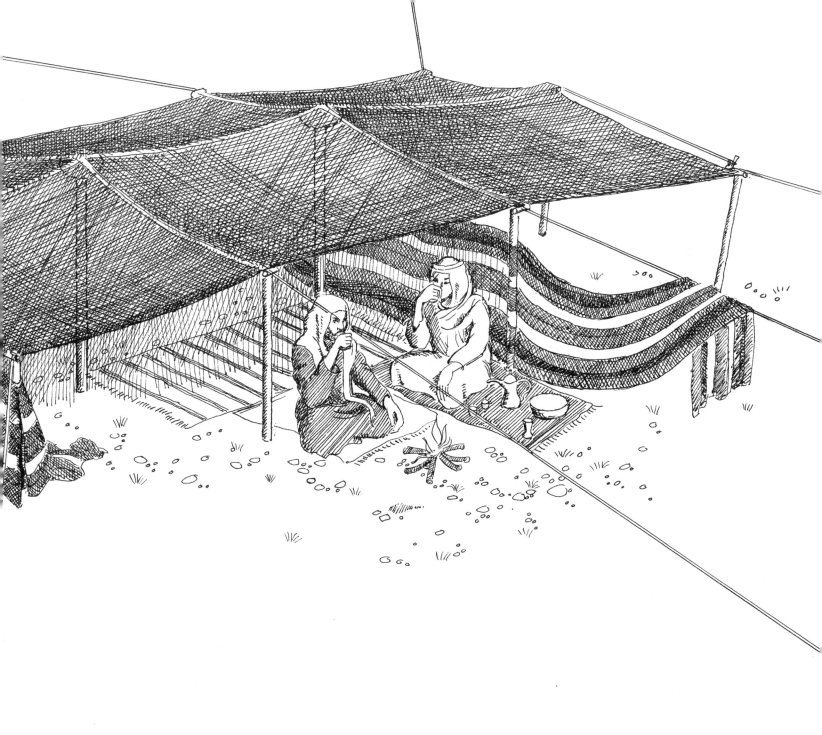

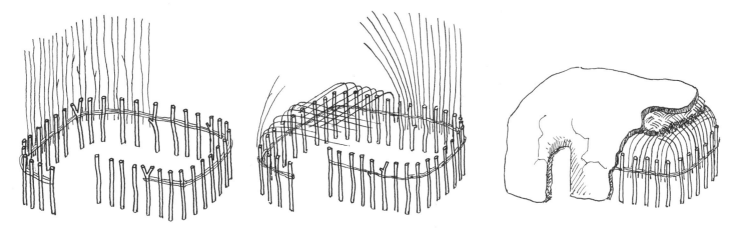

MASAI HUTS

In the grasslands of Kenya and Tanzania in East Africa, the Masai people raise cattle. All members of a Masai family—grandparents, fathers, mothers, brothers and sisters, children and cousins—move with their cattle whenever there is need for fresh grazing ground.

The Masai women build the shelters. As few as five or as many as fifty huts are built in a circle. The frame of the hut is usually made by setting long, flexible green sticks in a rectangle in the ground, and pulling the tops of the sticks together over a roof pole. In another method, sturdy posts are set into the ground and held in place by a crosspiece; then saplings are attached to one side and bent over to the opposite side to form the roof. Thick layers of grass are tied around the outside. Then the grass is plastered over with a mixture of mud and cow dung which dries into a hard covering.

There is a door made of cowhide and a small smoke hole, but no peepholes. It is dark inside. The huts are used only to sleep in or in rainy weather.

In the center of the circle of huts is a fenced place for the cattle to stay at night. A prickly thorn fence around the huts keeps out wild beasts, especially hyenas. This kind of settlement for people and their animals is known in Africa as a kraal. The men and boys take the cattle out and guard them while they graze all day. At sunset, the cattle are brought back to the kraal.

The Masai stay in one place until all the grass for some miles around has been eaten by the cattle. When this has happened, the family leaves the old huts and moves on to make another kraal in a new place.

BEMBA HUTS

Farther south, in Zambia, lie grassy plains where there are few trees. The Bemba people there make their houses with a wooden framework held together by mud. This kind of house building is called wattle and daub.

The first thing a Bemba builder has to do is find enough trees to make the frame for his house. He needs dozens of strong posts with sharpened ends. It might take him several months to collect enough. When he is ready, he begins by drawing a big circle on the ground, because this is going to be a round house. He digs a trench around the circle, sets the posts in place, fills the trench with earth, and stamps the earth down hard to keep the posts standing up straight.

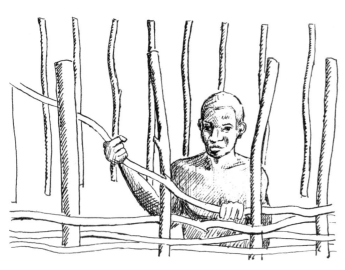

Now the builder takes flexible branches and weaves them in and out among the posts, around and around. He ties the branches to the posts with strips of wet bark that will shrink as they dry and hold everything tightly together. As he works on the frame of the house it begins to look like a basket with space left open for a little doorway. This framework is the wattle part.

Next the builder adds the daub. He makes a sticky mixture of clay and water and plasters it on the wattle frame, covering the whole outside. He smooths more daub over the inside. When dried by the sun, the walls are thick and solid.

Now the round house needs a roof. It is hard to make the roof alone, so friends come to help. A tall pole with a crosspiece is placed in the center of the house for workers to climb on. Everyone helps to tie saplings to the top of the pole with strips of wet bark. The saplings are spread out like the ribs of an umbrella and tied in place.

Bundles of long grass are tied onto the roof frame to make a thatch. When it is finished, the roof looks like a pointed hat with a topknot of grass.

The last thing to be made is a flat door of reeds tied together. Inside the house the family has sleeping mats, and overhead there are racks for storing food. The house is cool and dark to come into during the hot dry season. It is a snug house to be in during the time of year when it rains hard every day.

But ants and bugs like living in it too, and the wind begins to blow bits off the grass roof. In a few years it will be time to build a new wattle-and-daub house in a different place.

51

Mixing adobe

Adobe mold

NORTH AFRICAN ADOBE HOUSES

Other Africans who are not nomads make farm or village houses of adobe. If people live in the hot dry parts of Nigeria, Tunisia, or the Sudan, they may decide they want an adobe house.

The bricks are made of mud and water mixed with bits of straw and manure. Some builders make the bricks with their hands in the shape of balls or cones. Others make molds of wood and pour in the mud mixture. When the mud has hardened a bit, the brick is lifted out of the mold and put in the sun to dry for several days.

When enough bricks for a house have been made, a foundation trench is dug and rows of bricks are laid on top of each other. They are held together with a mortar of clay and lime.

Like the Pueblo Indian houses, many African adobe buildings have flat roofs. A flat roof makes a pleasant place for the family to sit or sleep during the cool evenings. Some houses are made with domed roofs. A domed roof may be built over a frame of wooden arches, or the

bricks may be put in place in a spiral, like the blocks of snow of an Eskimo igloo. A domed roof is harder to make than a flat one, but it looks beautiful and the rooms inside are high ceilinged and airy.

An adobe house in an African village or farm is often built around a courtyard, an open space without a roof in the center of the house. In this enclosed place open to the sky the family can work and play in private away from the noise and bustle of the street and the curious eyes of the neighbors.

Mud-brick houses are good for all kinds of weather. When the sun is blazing hot and bright, the thick walls keep out the heat and glare. In places where it gets cold and rainy in winter, the walls hold in the heat of a fire. But if it rains too hard, the mud bricks may begin to melt. Then when the sun shines again, new bricks have to be made to repair the house.

STONE HOUSES

Europe too has many kinds of climate. In countries like Italy, Greece, and Spain, where it is dry and sunny, houses are often made of mud brick as in Africa.

In some places, stones are used instead of bricks. On the rocky shores of Ireland or Norway, fishermen build snug houses of stone.

There are two ways to build with stone. One is to choose your stones very carefully so they will lie flat on top of each other. You lay out the first row of stones. Then you lay the next row above

that, fitting the stones with great care so they stay in place, and you continue fitting each row so that the stones are firm and balanced. You fill in the cracks with small stones. This is called a dry wall, and if it is well done it will stand for a very long time.

Another way to build with stone is to use mortar, a mixture of lime, sand, and water. You do not have to be so careful about the size and shape of each stone because the mortar will hold them together.

The builder will probably decide to make the stone house small and low, because stones are heavy to lift. After a straw thatch has been tied on over the roof frame, some flat stones may be placed along the edge to help hold the thatch in place.

A stone house with a fireplace is a cozy place to be when the wind blows and the cold fog rolls in from the sea.

Fire pit

EARLY EARTH LODGES

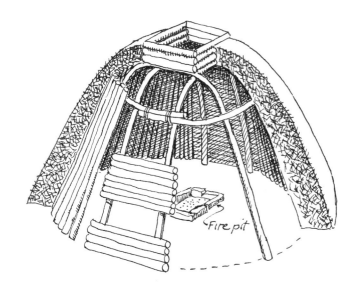

Fire pit

Northern Europe was once covered with dense forests, but the early inhabitants had only stone and bronze tools, which were not good for cutting down very large hardwood trees. Instead of living in houses made entirely of wood like the Northwest Coast Indians of North America, people built earth lodges. For this kind of shelter, a circular floor, about a foot deep, was dug in the ground and the dirt was packed down hard. Wooden posts held up roof beams and rafters. Everything was tied together with strips of wet leather or bark that tightened as they dried. Sticks were laid over the frame, then sod bricks—chunks of earth with grass and roots in them. The lodge looked like a low, grassy, flat-topped tent, with a doorway and a smoke hole. Such shelters were used throughout the lands that are now Germany, Scandinavia, and the British Isles.

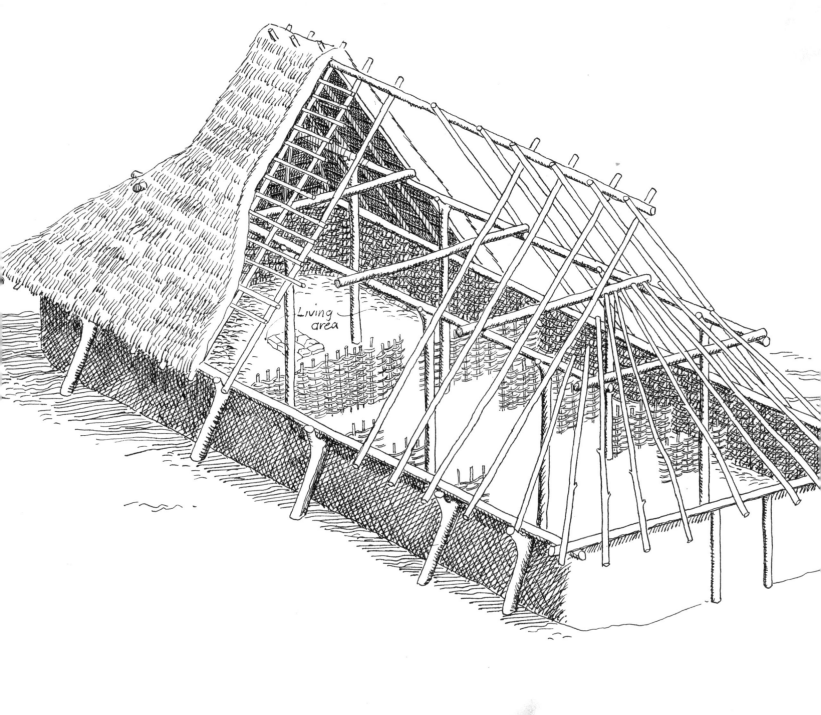

Living area

EARLY FARM HOUSES

An earth lodge was as warm and safe as an animal's den. But when people began farming, they needed more space. They needed places to store their hay and grain, and space to shelter their cows and sheep through the long winter. When iron tools were invented, about three thousand years ago, felling big trees and shaping wood became much easier. Now the builders could use heavy timbers. Log ends could be cut to fit into each other and be held by wooden pegs. The house frame could be rigid. It could be a square or a rectangle.

Walls were made of split logs or wattle and daub. End walls of the house could be shaped like triangles, from the roof line to the top, making a gable. Long rafters could stretch from one gable to the other, to support a slanted roof. Such a roof gave good storage space, and the snow slid easily off the steep sides. The roof was covered with a thick layer of straw thatch.

In Scandinavia, where the winters are very long and the snows heavy, wooden houses were made with flatter roofs and covered with sod.

The snow on top of the sod helped to keep the house and barn warm. In summer, the grass in the sod would grow and the roof would look like a little garden, all green and blossoming with bright flowers.

A strong wooden building like this could be added on to, making more space for animals and storage of grain. All over northern Europe, people have built sturdy wooden houses and barns like these and still build them today. Shelters built this way can last hundreds of years.

59

Almost everywhere on the planet Earth, people have found that they can live even in difficult climates. Depending upon where they are, fish and game will provide food, or people can grow grains, vegetables, and fruits and raise domestic animals. They have been able to make shelters which will protect them from heat or cold by using what is at hand.

In regions separated by great distances, some of the same kinds of shelters are built. Where they found big trees, the Indians of the Northwest Coast and the people of northern Europe built houses of wood. Where there are plants like bamboo, long grass or reeds, the people of New Guinea, Bali, South America, and Africa use them for their shelters. Animal skins and wool have been useful for the tipis of the Plains Indians, the yurts of the Kazaks, and the tents of Berbers and Bedouins. In Africa and northern Europe walls are made of wattle and daub. Stone is used wherever it is plentiful, as it is in Norway and Ireland. In dry regions, Pueblo Indians, Africans, and people of southern Europe all make adobe houses. Only the snow house is not found anywhere except in the Arctic.

Some kinds of simple shelters are no longer being built now that it is possible to get other materials. Many people have changed their old ways of living. But many others have not, and they still build the same kinds of shelters, huts, and houses that have been made for countless generations. Children still learn from their parents and grandparents how to find materials and use them for building. They still make good shelters without steel, concrete, glass, plastic, or any of the synthetics used in modern buildings. They still use simple tools and build without using energy except that which comes from the sun or their own muscles.

Now there are more people than ever before on earth, all needing food and shelter. Not everyone today lives where he can make good use of his own environment to provide food and shelter for himself and his family. But all of us can try to use the gifts of the earth wisely, as these builders of simple shelters have done for thousands of years before us.

GLOSSARY

adobe—a brick made of mud or clay dried in the sun

beam—a straight piece of wood stretching over a space from one wall to the other, strong enough to carry the weight above

brazier—an open pan for holding a small fire

courtyard—an uncovered space enclosed by the walls of a house

dome—a roof in the form of an upside-down cup

dung—solid body wastes of animals

fire pit—a shallow hole dug into the ground to hold a cooking fire

gable—the triangle made at the top of the end wall of a building between the two slopes of the roof

igloo—an Eskimo house; when it is made of snow blocks, it is a domed shape

kiva—an underground room in a Pueblo Indian village where the men hold secret meetings

kraal— a collection of African huts surrounded by a fence

lattice—an open screen or wall panel made of crossed strips of wood fastened together where they cross

long house—a house of poles covered with bark, large enough for several families, built by American Indians of the northeast and the eastern Great Lakes areas

maize—Indian corn

mesa—a flat-topped hill

monsoon—a wind which blows for six months, bringing rain to India and other parts of southern Asia

mortar—a mixture of sand and lime with water, used to hold together bricks or stones in walls

nomads—people who live by tending cattle or sheep and who move with their animals in search of pasture

paddy—a rice field

post—a strong piece of wood used as an upright support in building

pueblo—the Spanish word for village; an American Indian community of adobe or stone houses built together like apartments on mesas or flatlands of the Southwest

rafter—one of several sloping timbers supporting a roof

reed—a tall plant with a hollow, straight stem growing in a watery place

sapling—a young tree

sod—a piece of earth cut from the ground with grass still growing in it

steppes—grassy plains extending from southeastern Russia around the shores of the Caspian and Aral seas to the lowlands of Siberia

stilts—long wooden poles raising a house above the ground

thatch—a roof covering made of layers of straw, grass, reeds, or leaves

trench—a long narrow cut made by digging into the ground

tundra—flat swampy country at the edge of the Arctic circle, frozen most of the year

wattle and daub—a method of making a wall with interwoven sticks or twigs (wattle), plastered (daubed) with mud or clay

yurt—a circular tent-like dwelling constructed of skins and felt, stretched over a moveable framework, used by nomads of north and central Asia

About the Author

LEE PENNOCK HUNTINGTON has lived and worked in many parts of the world. She taught in Bogotá, Colombia, served on the Quaker Relief team in North Africa, and was a member of the Quaker representation at the United Nations in New York. She is the author of several children's books, including *Brothers in Arms* and *The Arctic and the Antarctic: What Lives There*. She presently reviews books for the Rutland, Vermont, *Daily Herald* and the Book-of-the-Month Club, and is Book Editor of *Country Journal*.

Mrs. Huntington is the mother of three children. She and her husband, an architect, live in Rochester, Vermont.

About the Illustrator

STEFEN BERNATH lives in New York City, where he is involved with many kinds of art projects, among them a popular series of nature coloring books. A graduate of Cooper Union, he has also worked in architectural offices and as a designer of record albums. For Coward, McCann & Geoghegan, Mr. Bernath has illustrated *Mountain Worlds: What Lives There* by Gilda Berger and *Spider Jane* by Jane Yolen.